North West Bus Memories in Colour
By Roger Hockney

Copyright IRWELL PRESS Ltd.,
978-1-906919-18-4
First published in 2010 by Irwell Press Ltd., 59A, High Street, Clophill, Bedfordshire, MK45 4BE
Printed by Konway Press

Everyone knows the significance of the year 1066 and, with luck, that of 1485 too. Few however will regard 1969 as having any meaning at all, yet a seismic shift was just about to get underway in the world of British bus transport. It would alter radically the character and scope of our bus services. Four factors would soon combine to change the nature of our bus fleets forever. First, the Transport Act 1968 would sweep away many municipal fleets in our metropolitan areas; secondly, one of our largest bus operators, British Electric Traction (BET), had decided to throw in the towel and sell out to the state owned Transport Holding Company (Tilling had already been thus absorbed) in 1969. This paved the way for wholesale rationalisation which reached its climax with the deregulation of services. Thirdly, car ownership was steadily rising. Customer diversion had started to bite for both bus operators and British Railways. Finally, the half cab bus was doomed by government legislation designed to promote one man operation, producing a bias towards the construction of rear engined buses.

So in the North West, by the end of 1969, the new Passenger Transport Authority for South East Lancashire and North East Cheshire, SELNEC, had swallowed up no less than eleven municipal transport undertakings and the Transport Holding Company had bought BET's transport interests. The Transport Holding Company was soon to metamorphose into the National Bus Company and the consequent rationalisation would, notably, spell the end for the North Western Road Car Company in 1972 while Ribble would be shorn of some of its peripheral operations. SELNEC itself was turned into the Greater Manchester PTE by 1974 as yet another local government reorganisation took place, following which in 1976 it swallowed up the largest remaining private operator, Lancashire United, which survived in name only, until 1981.

When I visited the North West in 1969 to take many of the photographs in this book, I little realised that I was recording the last gasp for many operators, their liveries and their traditional operations. I hope that these pictures provide a precious, perhaps sentimental, glimpse of a time gone by, of Morris Oxfords, the arrival of colour television, of duffel bags, gabardine macs and bus trips to the seaside.

A special thanks goes to Derrick Codling, for help with some of the background information, as well as photographic contributions to fill the inevitable gaps in my collection.
Roger Hockney, Lichfield 2010.

It's early July 1969 in Wigan and we're into the last few months for Wigan Corporation Transport as an independent undertaking. ACK 6B (No.3) is one of a batch of ten Massey-bodied front entrance Leyland Titan PD2/27As, delivered in 1964. Wigan's fleet numbering was random, since it was the practice to simply fill any gaps in the numbering system caused by withdrawals.

NORTH WEST BUS MEMORIES in COLOUR

Wigan Corporation No.62, EJP 504, squeezes past a Morris Minor as it proceeds on the No.22 service to Marsh Green in July 1969. A 1959 built Leyland PD3/2 bodied by local company Massey, it carries like all Wigan buses two green lights, one either side of the front destination indicator, a useful way for passengers to identify an approaching Wigan Corporation service at night in an area served by a variety of bus companies.

Wigan's front entrance Leyland Titan No.139, DEK 2D, rests between duties in Wigan on 5 July 1969. Since 1929, Wigan had only taken Leyland Motors products, which is not surprising given the town's proximity to the Leyland Motor works.

NORTH WEST BUS MEMORIES in COLOUR

Wheatsheaf Motors of Merthyr Tydfil didn't bother too much about repainting its second-hand acquisitions. Here's JP 8303, a former Wigan 56 seat all Leyland Titan PD2/1, built in 1950, but by June 1969 serving the residents of Merthyr and adjacent towns.

NORTH WEST BUS MEMORIES in COLOUR

Wigan Bus Station plays host to two of Ribble's familiar full fronted Leyland PD3/5s, both with attractive MCW bodywork. A year separates the two buses; PCK 362 (No1721) was built in 1961 and RCK 943 (No 1798) a year later. No.1721 is setting off for the run to Southport and its sister is heading for Ormskirk, on a sunny day in 1969. Ribble, sold with BET's other UK bus operations to the state owned Transport Holding Company in 1968, was based in Preston. It was one of the larger constituents of the BET Group, operating in excess of 1,000 buses from 28 garages in the North West. Only the mighty Midland Red was larger.

NORTH WEST BUS MEMORIES in COLOUR

Ribble was almost exclusively a patron of Leyland buses. In 1964 and 1965 it took delivery of 16 Albion Lowlanders with Alexander 72 seat bodies. Here's UCK 855 (No.1855) loading up at Wigan bus station for a run to Blackpool in July 1969. Albion only built 35 Lowlanders in these two years so doubtless Ribble's order kept a fairly thin production line going a little longer. Only six more were built before production ceased on what was a bit of a disaster of a bus. Leyland didn't want to build it, but Scottish operators preferred it to the new-fangled rear engined Atlantean, the early models of which were not that reliable. The Lowlander had technical problems and the design was not particularly attractive. It was assembled in Glasgow from parts manufactured at Leyland. That top deck front seat passengers sat higher to give the driver headroom suggests something of a makeshift quality to the design. Ribble had been absorbed into the newly formed state owned Transport Holding Company along with other BET Companies in 1968. This allowed consequent incorporation, along with Tilling Group bus interests, into the National Bus Company and eventual ownership, albeit in a divided form, by the Stagecoach Group.

Lancashire United Transport was a long-time buyer of Guy Arabs. Here's Guy Arab IV, 141 NTF (No 50) built in 1960 with Wigan-based Northern Counties 73 seat bodywork at Wigan bus station in July 1969, heading for Bolton. By this time LUT was the largest independent bus operator in England and Wales with 400 vehicles.

A pleasing study of a Lancashire United Northern Counties-bodied Guy Arab IV, basking in the sun at Bolton bus station in July 1969. Lancashire United was acquired by Greater Manchester PTE on 1 January 1976 and operated as a subsidiary under its existing name until being fully absorbed on 31 March 1981.

Bolton Corporation's Leyland Titan PD3/4 No.118 (MBN 173) awaits its next journey from Bolton to Harwood on a late afternoon in July 1969. Built in 1958, it has a 74 seat East Lancs bodywork. Bolton was yet another big buyer of Leyland buses.

Bury Corporation was another Council which acquired many Leyland Titans in the 1940s and 1950s, but by the 1960s turned its attention to rear engined Atlanteans and Fleetlines. Here's a relatively new Daimler Fleetline at Bolton bus station in July 1969.

Bury's livery was particularly attractive on their Leyland Titans. GEN 210 (No.210) was a PD3/6 from 1958. It has Weymann bodywork with rear entrance doors. It's reached Bolton (hence the proliferation of Bolton buses in the background) and will shortly be returning to Bury on the No.23 service; July 1969.

NORTH WEST BUS MEMORIES in COLOUR

Buses meet at Rochdale in July 1969. Ribble Atlantean NCK 351 (No.1610) was part of one of the earliest batches of PDR1/1 Atlanteans delivered to Ribble in 1959. It has MCW 78 seat bodywork and is heading towards Preston, while Bury Corporation's Daimler Fleetline in the background is ready to depart for its home town.

Rochdale Corporation shunned Leyland and was very much a buyer of AEC and Daimler buses. This is a very smart looking Gardner engined AEC Regent V D2RA6G, bodied by Weymann. NDK 975 (No.275) was built in 1956 and was 13 years old at the time the photograph was taken in Rochdale; the ivory and blue livery sets it off to good effect.

Rochdale's first rear engined buses came in a delivery of twelve Daimler Fleetlines in 1964 and 1965. Here's EDK 129C (No.329) of the later batch, bodied by Weymann, leaving Rochdale for Ashton in July 1969. Two AEC Regent Vs await departure behind it.

Leyland Titan PD2/40 UNB 549 (No.3549) was one of a large number of Leyland Titan variants in the Manchester fleet. It carries Metro-Cammell bodywork and was built in 1958. It's leaving Rochdale in 1969 and heading back to Manchester Piccadilly on what must be a warm July day; the driver has rolled up the sleeves of this jacket.

NORTH WEST BUS MEMORIES in COLOUR

A July summer evening in Rochdale in 1969 and an illustration of the overlapping nature of bus services in the North West. Ashton-under-Lyne No.32 (332 TF) was a 1963 Roe-bodied Leyland Titan PD2/40. It's heading for Stalybridge whilst the following Oldham Leyland Titan is en route for Wernath. A North Western Leyland Atlantean is picking up passengers opposite.

North Western was a purchaser of Dennis Lolines, such as this Loline II in Stockport, heading for Mellor in July 1969. RDB 815 (No.815) was built in 1960 and has East Lancs front entrance bodywork. It was part of a relatively large (for Dennis) batch of fifteen buses for North Western, mostly with Leyland engines. (Three had Gardner 6LX engines). In fact only 45 Lolines were built in 1960. Essentially, the Loline was a Bristol Lodekka built under licence and North Western was the largest purchaser (buying fifty) after Aldershot and District. The Telefusion and Visionhire shops are promoting TV sets with BBC2 *and* colour reception!

NORTH WEST BUS MEMORIES in COLOUR

In the 1960s, derelict land such as bomb sites was often used for bus parking. A varied group of North Western vehicles, from the AEC, Daimler and Leyland stables await their next turns of duty at their Stockport headquarters in July 1969. A BET Group company, like sister Ribble, the North Western Road Car Company was operating over 500 buses at this time around the southern flanks of Manchester and to Buxton, Crewe, Warrington and Macclesfield. Its longer distance services reached Derby, Sheffield and seaside resorts. The BET controlled fleets were sold to the state owned Transport Holding Company in 1968, thus allowing the new National Bus Company to be formed. So this picture in 1969 represents a transition period for the fleet. It was all change again in 1972 when on 1 January SELNEC PTE acquired North Western from NBC and expunged the name.

Leyland built its last Titans in 1969 when this picture was taken at Stockport bus station. This Stockport version, KJA 882F, is only a year old but still looks dated beside the rear engined Fleetlines and Atlanteans which had been on the road since, surprisingly, 1956 when the Atlantean prototype entered service as a demonstrator. The conductor and driver are having a breather before setting off for Reddish. A North Western Dennis Loline lurks at the rear.

The gloriously named Stalybridge, Hyde, Mossley and Dukinfield Transport and Electricity Board operated a sizable fleet of buses between the aforementioned towns. A buyer principally of Leylands and Daimlers, it surprised the bus world in 1955 with the acquisition of the unique Atkinson centre entrance double decker, now preserved in Manchester's Museum of Transport. SHMD (as they were better known) was Britain's last operator to purchase centre entrance buses. More mundanely, here's one of the company's Leyland Atlanteans, in the Committee's rather dowdy livery, outside Stockport's Merseyway shopping centre, then under construction, in July 1969.

J. Fishwick and Sons operated in the Preston, Chorley and Leyland area. The buses were always well turned out, as demonstrated here by an immaculate Leyland Titan, 529 CTF, waiting to leave Preston in July 1969. Fast forward to the present and the company remains staunchly independent, running both stage and coach services with a fleet of almost fifty buses.

NORTH WEST BUS MEMORIES in COLOUR

Preston in July 1969 and the driver, out of his cab, seems to be suggesting that the lady in the red coat has stepped in something nasty. The conductress leans against the wall, chatting. Meanwhile Preston Corporation Leyland Titan PD3/5 MCK 295 (No.64) awaits a special duty. It's a 1958 built Leyland with seventy seat front entrance Metro-Cammell bodywork in the Corporation's former crimson and cream livery. The new blue and cream order, introduced around 1967, is displayed across the road. Preston moved to front entrances with this batch of seven buses. It was an exclusively Leyland purchaser, predictably.

No.84 (TRN 386) is in Preston Corporation's revised livery, but surprisingly the Council still made little attempt to advertise its ownership, preferring a tiny Preston crest inscribed with its motto *Proud Preston*; but at least the blue colour lifts the appearance of the bus. It's a Leyland Titan PD3A/1, the first of seven such vehicles delivered in 1964 with Metro-Cammell seventy seat bodywork. It's leaving Preston and heading to the suburb of Ribbleton on a July 1969 afternoon.

Preston's earlier rear entrance vehicles benefitted visually from the new colour scheme. Here's No.126 (DRN 309) which was an all Leyland product. This 56 seat PD2/1 was built in 1950 and is standing outside the civic buildings in July 1969. Preston Corporation continued to operate public transport services until 1993, when an employee buyout was agreed.

Blackburn Corporation's buses were always smartly turned out. Indeed, an inverse law seemed to operate; the older they were, the smarter they looked. This 1949-built Guy Arab III 6LW (CBV 436) was twenty years old when photographed at Blackburn's bus station. You either loved or hated the somewhat quirky, but definitely distinctive Crossley bodywork, which was relatively unusual on a Guy chassis. These 25 Guy Arab IIIs, delivered in 1949, gave an average of 23 years' service. The last went in 1973.

Blackburn Corporation was a buyer of Leyland Titans and Guy Arabs in more or less equal numbers. Two Arab IV 6LWs await passengers at the bus station. The nearer is HCB 143 (No.143) built in 1958 with East Lancs bodywork. The year of this photograph (1969) marked the end of Guy Arab production. The Corporation Transport undertaking was to survive until 2006, when it was sold to Lancashire United, the second company to be thus named.

It's 5.15pm and workers in Blackburn wait for buses home under an advertisement for Belle Vue Zoo, but Darwen Corporation's service is passing them by. It ran a fleet of about thirty-five buses, predominantly Leyland Titans; this one is FTD 249B, a PD3A/1 with East Lancs front entrance bodywork. It was one of two delivered in 1964. The Corporation must have been happy with them since three more arrived a year later. Darwen Corporation Transport disappeared in 1974, a result of local government reorganisation when, as some might say, it was swallowed up by Blackburn Corporation.

Accrington Corporation buses benefitted from a very pleasant livery of dark blue and red. It was another smartly turned out fleet. Here's 825 KTB, a 1959 Guy Arab IV 6LW with a sister parked to the rear. The bodywork is by East Lancs. The Corporation, like neighbouring Blackburn, liked the Guy product which was not always the cheapest of buses available, although it still found the opportunity to buy home-grown Leyland Titans.

Rossendale Joint Transport Committee was formed on 1 April 1968 by the amalgamation of the fleets operated by Haslingden and Rawtenstall Corporations. Such was the inter-relationship of their operations that they had shared the same General Manager since 1949. Ramsbottom Corporation shared the same Manager too and had also considered joining up, but thought better of it. FTE 633B is still carrying its Rawtenstall fleet number a year after amalgamation. It's one of an all Leyland fleet, a five year old PD3/4 Titan and one of four with front entrance East Lancs bodywork, dating from 1964. It's leaving Accrington for the run to Bacup via Rawtenstall, the main trunk service for the fleet. Rossendale survives today as an 'arms length' company linked to Rossendale Borough Council.

Accrington Corporation bought Guy Arabs and Leyland Titans in almost equal numbers. CTB 557B is a Guy Arab V 6LW built in 1964 with East Lancs rear entrance bodywork. By 1967, they had moved to purchasing front entrance Leyland Titans, one of which, across the road, awaits departure from Accrington, for Clayton.

An Austin Cambridge slips past Burnley Colne and Nelson Joint Transport Committee's Leyland Titan PD2/12. Fourteen years old at the time of this photograph, it is one of a batch of 24 buses built between 1953 and 1956. An East Lancs bodied version, it went into service in 1955. It's parked at Burnley bus station; BCN was a Leyland supporter, apart from a brief lapse in 1951 when it bought some Guy Arabs. The fleet was renamed Burnley and Pendle upon local government reorganisation in 1974 and finally lost its independent existence, being sold to Stagecoach, before being reborn as Burnley and Pendle under its next owner in 2001.

Todmorden Joint Omnibus Committee, formed in 1931, was a joint venture between Todmorden Corporation and British Railways. Each bus was owned by either partner. No.7 (KWX 12) was owned by the Corporation. It was already 18 years old when photographed in 1969 and certainly looks its age, which is exacerbated by the somewhat drab olive green livery and old fashioned split destination blind. Like all the fleet, it was a Leyland product, being a 1951 Titan PD2/12 fitted with Leyland 53 seat bodywork. It's leaving Burnley for Todmorden and Hebden Bridge. Another quirk of this fleet was the use of random numbers, filling gaps in the sequence arising from withdrawn vehicles. Older vehicles were often placed in a duplicate list, with an X added to the existing fleet number.

Chester Corporation loved Guy Arabs. Most of their fleet came from that manufacturer, including some of the last of them to be built. Here's a 1954 Guy Arab IV in historic Chester, unusually bodied by Guy on Park Royal frames, in July 1969.

Chester Corporation Guy Arab V 6LW picking up at The Rows in Chester in July 1969. Delivered in 1965, it has Massey front entrance 75 seat bodywork. Massey had gone by 1967, taken over by Wigan neighbour Northern Counties. Chester's bus livery was originally green and cream, until Chester-based Crosville abandoned maroon in the war years and adopted Tilling's corporate green and cream livery. Chester Corporation promptly revised its livery to maroon!

Bristol Lodekka production had ceased in 1968, one year before Crosville Bristol Lodekka FS6B 4213 FM was caught loading a Mold service in Chester. By 1969 Bristol was two years into building the rear engined VRT but Crosville was not tempted and concentrated on buying large numbers of rear engined single deckers. This Lodekka has, like all Lodekkas, an Eastern Coachwork body, but is also fitted with Cave-Browne-Cave heating, which can be identified by the radiators on either side of the destination blind. Crosville was swallowed up by the National Bus Company, which itself was split up in due course, thus obliterating the name of this large and geographically widespread operator.

It's 1969 and time for a break in Leigh. The crew of Lancashire United Daimler Fleetline No.175 look on as a Leigh Corporation AEC Renown, 3B3RA PTC 113C, is snapped. Immediate sister PTC 114C is preserved at the Museum of Transport in Manchester. Leigh bought predominantly AEC vehicles, but dabbled with both Leyland Titans and Dennis Lolines. All double deckers in its fleet had low bridge or low height bodies because of a low entrance to the bus depot (poor planning there!). The Renown was built in 1965 and bodied by East Lancs. Why two fleet numbers are required at the front end is anyone's guess. The Lancashire United Daimler Fleetline is a 1964 Northern Counties product.

In 1965 East Lancs delivered a batch of twelve Leyland PD2/40 specials to Warrington Corporation with 7ft 6in wide bodywork. BED 733C (No.52) was the last of the batch. It is parked outside a vintage Tesco in Warrington in the summer of 1969, before leaving for Dallam. The fleet survived in local government ownership until 1986, when it was converted to an 'arms length' company, wholly owned by Warrington Council.

A dull summer day at Salford's Victoria bus station in 1969 and two of Salford's Leyland Titans await their next jobs. The nearer one is a 1964-built PD2/40 with front entrance Metro-Cammell bodywork; the other is a similar 1966 version. By this time, Salford Corporation also used Fleetlines and Atlanteans, but old habits die hard and front engine vehicles were still seen as reliably filling the bill.

Morecambe and Heysham Corporation Transport was to be swallowed up by Lancaster Corporation upon local government reorganisation in 1974 and that time is approaching fast as Morecambe's Leyland Titan PD2/37, 33 WTD (No.87) whizzes the No.1 service along the promenade past the Cyclone towards Heysham in September 1973. Built in 1960, it carries a front entrance Massey body. Morecambe's fleet was relatively old and so, predictably, most of its buses disappeared rapidly after the Lancaster takeover.

Morecambe and Heysham No.79 (TTB 688) is a 1954 Park Royal bodied AEC Regent III 6812A. It's pottering along the promenade in September 1973, its destination being the delightfully named Morecambe suburb of Bare.

Barrow Corporation operated a smart all-Leyland fleet. Here at the Hindpool Road depot we find two Leyland Titan variants basking in the sun on a May day in 1976. HEO 272 nearer the camera is a 1961 Massey-bodied front entrance PD2A/27, whilst tucked away is PD2/40, a Park Royal product of 1958. The blue and cream livery was introduced way back in 1930.

There's not a lot of road traffic in Barrow in Furness in May 1976 as Leyland Titan PD2A/27 HEO 279 passes by heading for Walney Island. It's a Massey bodied vehicle with a 64 seat front entrance body. In the late 1980s, Barrow Corporation Transport was absorbed by the Stagecoach Group.

Blackpool Corporation was enamoured of Leyland. Here are two of its Metro Cammell bodied Leyland Titan PD3/As, built in 1967 and 1968 respectively. They were part of Blackpool's last order for such buses, almost at the end of the Titans' production run. Between them we see a Fylde Borough Metro Cammell-bodied Leyland Atlantean No.92 (acquired second-hand from the Merseyside PTA) in Blackpool in 1980. The Titans had eight years life left. Fylde Borough continued to operate buses until its fleet was amalgamated with Blackpool Transport in 1994.

Llandudno Urban District Council operated a small fleet of buses for the tourist trade. By 1981, this 1954 Guy Otter with Roe bodywork was in the red and grey livery of Aberconwy District Council and at 27 years of age was still providing tours around the area.

NORTH WEST BUS MEMORIES in COLOUR

The wartime 'make do and mend' ethos still survived in the 1960s. Manchester Corporation's Leyland Tiger TS2 No.28, dating from 1930, is still earning its keep as a staff canteen at Chorlton Street bus station in April 1964. What the roof top excrescence might be can only be guessed at – ventilation for the steaming kettles, a water tank? Photograph Derrick Codling.

Is the Bare Lane level crossing (behind us) closed to road traffic, since Morecambe and Heysham's AEC Regent III on the Heysham Village service hasn't pulled away from the Bare Lane Station stop? The conductor is having a chat to the driver. KTF 587 (No.58) is one of Morecambe and Heysham's venerable Regent IIIs, built in 1949 and bodied by Park Royal. It took five years to supply this batch of 26 vehicles. The period is August 1964. Photograph Derrick Codling.

St Helens Corporation Leyland PD2/A RDJ 732 (L32) rests outside the bus depot at St Helens, in November 1965. It was built in 1962 and carries an East Lancs body. In the distance we see TDJ 610 (No 210) one of five Marshall bodied AEC Reliance 2MU3 RA buses built between 1963 and 1965. Sister No.612 is preserved in the North West Museum of Road Transport at St Helens. The prefix letter attached to fleet numbers related to the batches of Transport Committee purchases. Photograph Derrick Codling.

Liverpool Corporation's D518 (JKC 143) was only months away from withdrawal when this photograph was taken at The Pier Head in January 1965. Looking older than its sixteen years, it's a Daimler CVA6 with Northern Counties bodywork. By now it was one of the last of a batch of ninety Daimler buses with either AEC engines, designated CVA6, or Daimler engines, designated CVD6. Northern Counties shared the bodywork construction contract with Weymann. Beyond it, we see parked one of Liverpool's unpainted aluminium bodied Leyland Titan PD2/30 buses, built by Crossley in 1961. There's what looks to be an AEC Regent V in the background with what appears to be an illegal passenger on the roof! Photograph Derrick Codling.

Southport Corporation had sold this 1947 all-Leyland Titan PD2/3 by May 1965 to Holmeswood Coaches when it was caught in Church Row, Chorley, operating a Euxton Royal Ordnance Factory Workers' service. Formerly No.92 (FFY 409), its sisters survived a little longer with Southport as open top seafront buses. Photograph Derrick Codling.

It's the end of the shift at Euxton Royal Ordnance Factory near Chorley with Ribble and Bolton Corporation buses turning out on workers' special services. Ribble No.2485 is an interesting Leyland Titan PD2/3. Originally with a Brush body, it was one of 22 buses remodelled with eight feet wide lowbridge bodies by Burlingham. It is soon to be withdrawn. Bolton's Leyland Titan is probably a 1961 PD2/27. The bus advertising is competing for smokers' custom. Photograph Derrick Codling.

Lancaster City Transport No.571 (HTF 571) looks very smart. It is a 1947 Crossley DD42/5, with fine Crossley bodywork. It's standing at the bus station, having been on the Beaumont Estate service via Slyne Road, in August 1965. Photograph Derrick Codling.

You wait ages for a bus, then they come along in fives! In this case, it's August 1965 and Lancaster City Transport buses are heading along Westgate towards Morecambe bus depot. They will load the crowds leaving the illuminations in Happy Mount Park at Morecambe and take them to view the lights along the promenade, before returning to Lancaster garage. Leader of the pack is 202 YTE, a 1963 Leyland Titan, followed by sister 201 YTE. Further down the line we find a couple of 1951, all Leyland Titans. No.201 has survived into preservation at the North West Museum of Road Transport at St Helens. Photograph Derrick Codling.

Morecambe and Heysham Corporation veterans stand opposite the promenade at the Battery in Morecambe in August 1965. No.25, CTB 64, is an AEC Regent 0661 built in 1938 and bodied by Park Royal, subsequently being converted to an open topper. No.15 (CTJ 696) is a 1947 Regent II 0661/20, again with Park Royal bodywork. The Council certainly liked to get its moneys worth from its buses. The youngest was already 18 years old when this photo was taken. The hoarding advertises the season's exciting shows on the Central Pier. Photograph Derrick Codling.

NORTH WEST BUS MEMORIES in COLOUR

Ribble's first purchase of Leyland underfloor buses was the Leyland Olympic in 1951. DRN 136 (No.272) was one of thirty on Ribble's books. The Weymann front entrance bodywork accommodated 44 passengers. It is seen here at Bowness Pier on the short 549 service from Windermere. By this time, August 1965, withdrawals were already making inroads into the fleet. Photograph Derrick Codling.

Following a crunch with a car in Scale Hall Lane in August 1965, Lancaster City Transport No.175 (175 FTJ) has been left by its driver while he is in conversation with the car driver. It's one of five Leyland Tiger Cub PSUC1/3 buses with East Lancs bodywork acquired in 1958 and 1959. This one was sold by 1968. The No.4 Service was operated jointly with Ribble. Curiously, both companies used different names for the same destination on this service. Ribble called it service L4 between Lancaster and Penryhn Road. Lancaster City Transport called it the No.4 service from the Town Hall in Dalton Square to Cross Hill! Photograph Derrick Codling.

Manchester trolleybus operations were on the wane when this photograph was taken on a wet day in September 1965. ONE 742 and ONE 749 were part of a large batch of BUT 9612T buses with Burlingham bodywork acquired in 1955. They are on service 218 from Piccadilly to Stalybridge. Withdrawals were already making inroads into the fleet, being a precursor to the total closure of the trolleybus network with little ceremony at the end of December 1966. Photograph Derrick Codling.

Ashton-under-Lyne shared trolleybus services with Manchester and here's one of their eight BUT 9612T buses (built in 1956 with Bond bodywork) in Manchester on the joint 218 service to Stalybridge in September 1965. Predictably, all the Ashton trolleybuses were also withdrawn at the end of December 1966, when the Manchester system closed. Photograph Derrick Codling.

Ribble's Leyland Tiger Cub FCK 843 (No.411) dates from 1954. It has arrived at Glasson Dock with a service from Lancaster in April 1966. There were fifty of these buses, which had some of the last bodies built by Saunders Roe before it ceased trading. Converted to one man operation in the late 1950s, all had left Ribble's service by 1969. Photograph Derrick Codling.

Ribble's 1850 (TCK 850) was the last of a batch of 131 Leyland PD3/5 buses supplied with MCW 72 seat front entrance bodies over a period from 1961 to 1963. For the next twenty years they became the iconic Ribble bus, with the last examples finally leaving the fleet in 1981. This one is operating the L6 Heysham-Morecambe-Lancaster service in February 1967. Photograph Derrick Codling.

In March 1967 Lancaster City Transport was still operating this 1943 Guy Arab II 5LW. FTD 727 lost its wartime utility body in 1952, when it was replaced by Park Royal. It's at Lancaster bus station, resting between duties. Lancaster's fleet numbering was at the time based on registration numbers, so this is not the 727th vehicle in the fleet! Later, double deck buses were numbered in the 200 series. Photograph Derrick Codling.

Two year old Weymann-bodied Leyland Leopard PSU3/1R ARN 562B (No.562) pulls away from Ribblehead en route for Ingleton in 1967; the Settle and Carlisle railway line is in the background. Ribble service 483 was not one of its most profitable and, operating between Ingleton and Hawes via Ribblehead, passenger loadings were, as this photograph shows, decidedly light. In fact, with a conductor on board, there were more staff than passengers on this working. Photograph Derrick Codling.

Former Ribble vehicles didn't fade away, they were sold to the Ulster Transport Authority; making the point, two all-Leyland Royal Tigers of 1952 look decidedly the worst for wear in May 1967, at an unidentified location in the province. Formerly 374 and 398 in the Ribble fleet, they were sold to the UTA in the mid-1960s, to become 9018 and 9034 in the UTA fleet. Photograph Derrick Codling.

Douglas Corporation AEC Regent 0661, No.50, was a Northern Counties-bodied specimen dating from 1939, one of the first diesel engined buses in the fleet. DMN 650 is pictured in Douglas at the unique Derby Castle transport interchange between buses, horse trams and the Manx Electric Tramway, in July 1967. Photograph Derrick Codling.

NORTH WEST BUS MEMORIES in COLOUR

We're in Whitehaven on a dull September day in 1969 and Cumberland all Leyland PD2 LRM186 (No.332) of 1952 rests before setting off on a local town service. Behind, an Austin Cambridge overtakes one of Cumberland's Bristol Lodekkas. Cumberland was acquired by the Tilling Group in 1942. Prior to that it was principally an operator of Leyland buses, a habit that continued well into its Tilling days, as opposed to purchasing the Tilling Group's obligatory Bristol products. Photograph Derrick Codling.